Pottery on the Wheel for Beginners

By Steve McDonald

Table of Contents

Introduction

Welcome to beginning pottery on the wheel. Whether this is your first time touching clay, or it is just your first time using a pottery wheel, this book is designed to teach you everything you need to know to get started.

Learn how to throw pots, fire and glaze your projects. Also learn to choose the best ceramics supplies, tools, wheels, clay and kilns.

You'll find easy to follow lessons, including photos, and step by step instructions for making pottery mugs, bowls and vases.

Learning to use the wheel is challenging, but the rewards are great.

There is nothing like eating or drinking out of a pot that you've created yourself.

Have you ever watched someone making a pot on the wheel and felt like it was just magical?

Have you been dreaming forever of making your own pots in a studio all your own?

If so, this book can teach you the basic skills you need to begin creating your own magic on the pottery wheel.

Here is what you'll learn in this book...

- How to throw pottery on the wheel
- The life of a ceramic pot from clay to green ware to bisque to glaze
- Decorating clay pots with glaze
- Firing clay projects
- Setting up your own ceramics studio
- Functional beginning projects.
- Photos and lessons to guide you through your first pots.
- Tips, tricks, and techniques throughout.

First, let me tell you briefly why I started teaching.

The first time I tried making a pot it was a disaster. I was in the ninth grade. I tried every day for five straight days. All I made were mud pies.

It was so frustrating. It seemed impossible. I had always been good at drawing and painting. I couldn't see why this would be any different.

The problem was that I had no one to show me how.

Out of frustration I quit. I didn't try again for four years.

I desperately needed a teacher.

Finally, while in college, I signed up for a beginning wheel throwing class. There, I found an awesome teacher.

Watching her throw pottery was magical.

HUGE POTS sprang out of raw clay in her hands. She made it look so easy. I was inspired.

Over the next several years she taught me to make more than mud pies.

I learned how to make everything, from mugs to vases and teapots.

Now I absolutely love making pots on the wheel.

The important thing I learned is that **anyone can make pottery** with the right teaching and techniques.

That includes YOU!

You don't need a college degree or expensive lessons.

You just need a teacher. Inspired by my first teacher, I started teaching my own students ten years ago.

Since then I have taught hundreds of people how to make ceramics.

Now, I'd like to teach YOU.

So, if you're ready to make your own handmade bowls, mugs, vases and more, **let's begin**.

Chapter 1 - Getting Started

What does it take to learn how to make pottery on the wheel? Here are the three pillars of pottery making.

Also, below are five essential supplies to get you started.

Pottery Defined - Pottery is the process of forming pots (bowls, cups, vases and more) out of wet clay, then firing it in an oven to make it hard and usable.

The Three Pillars of Pottery

1) Supplies

2) Instruction

3) Patience

The first two, Supplies and Instruction , can be found right in this book. Keep reading for more information.

The third element, Patience, you have to bring to the equation. The hardest part about learning how to make pottery is the initial learning hump.

You will probably need about 20-30 attempts before you are proficient at centering clay and making a bowl. From that point the sky is the limit as you expand your skill into more advanced projects like coffee mugs, vases, teapots and more.

The hardest part, however, is getting over that initial hump. If you can remember to be patient, have fun with learning, and keep trying you'll enjoy pottery and be able to take it as far as you want.

So, with that being said, let's learn more about it....

People make pottery for a variety of reasons; as a fun hobby, to express their creativity, to make functional pots for use around the house. Many people even become full-time, professional pottery artists.

Pottery making varies from forming tiny pinch pots by hand to making intricate works of art for galleries or museums. This site is dedicated to teaching you how to make functional pottery on the electric pottery wheel. Before we get started, we'll need to get prepared....

Five Essentials to Making Pottery

1. A Pottery Studio Space

This is just a space to put yourself, your tools and your wheel. It could be a garage, a basement a spare room, or the corner of your kitchen. Don't have much space? There are lots of creative ways to turn a cramped space into a great studio.

2. A Kick or Electric Pottery Wheel

Wheels come in many variations. The main types are kick wheels and electric wheels. Some wheels are large and weigh hundreds of pounds, while others are small enough to be used on a table and stored under the bed when not in use.

3. Pottery Clay

Clay is the magical, sticky, yet solid substance that you form the pots out of. In its wet form it can be molded and re-molded. It will hold its shape after forming. It is soft when wet and gets stiffer as it dries.

4. Tools and other Pottery Supplies

A few basic hand tools are all you need: a sponge, a knife, a cutting wire, a cutting needle, and a hard scraping rib will do.

5. Access to Ceramic Kilns

A kiln is basically just a heat source for cooking your clay pot. It bakes the moisture out of the clay and melts the clay just enough to fuse the clay particles together, making it very hard and permanent. Kilns use different types of fuel to make the heat including gas, wood, and electricity. Most towns have a store or school where you can fire your pottery if you don't have your own kiln.

Setting Up a Pottery Studio

I need a pottery studio. How do I set one up?

It's the burning question for many aspiring potters. This is your guide to setting up your own space on any budget in any location.

There are lots of options to choose from when considering where to make your own pottery. Many pottery artists use ceramics facilities at art schools or stores where ceramic art supplies are sold.

These are a great way to get started, but eventually, **you're going to want a pottery space to call your own.**

Over the course of my career **I've used many different spaces to create pottery**... anywhere from friends' garages to empty corners of a bedroom (this requires a VERY supportive spouse).

11

Therefore, I know a lot of great tricks for creating a studio in a tight space on a tight budget.

Let's see what a "Perfect Pottery Studio" would look like, and then I'll share some tips on how to customize YOUR studio to fit your space, budget, and pottery needs.

The perfect studio would consist of a large room with a well organized work space. It would contain a convenient water source and a good utility sink.

If you have a room without water, that's okay. Click the link above for tips on how to use water without having a sink.

Of course no perfect pottery studio would be complete without **the perfect pottery wheel to suit your needs.** You can build, buy or borrow a pottery kick wheel or an electric pottery wheel.

It would also contain a wide variety of useful pottery tools, more on this later.

The organization of the tools will make a big difference in the efficiency of your work. A well-placed wedging table along with one or two other sturdy tables will provide convenient work spaces. This allows you to use a wider variety of techniques in your work.

Several pieces of equipment such as a slab roller and a pug mill can increase productivity while decreasing your own physical efforts. These are great to have, but are not necessary unless you are creating very large quantities of work.

I like to have several sturdy shelves and plastic bins for storage of projects in different stages of completion.

Storage is also important for organizing supplies such as pottery clay, glazes, pyrometric cones, and other tools.

Finally, you'll need a space for a kiln or at least a small hobby kiln. This can be the corner of a basement, a patio or an outdoor shop or garage.

Note: Always follow the manufacturer's safety recommendations for setting up your kiln.

How to Select the Perfect Electric Pottery Wheel

Choosing an electric pottery wheel to buy can be a daunting task.

We'll make it easier by finding answers to these important questions:

What features do I need?

How much should I pay?

What should I avoid at all costs?

Below are the answers to these questions and more.

Follow the discussion to choose the perfect attributes for your perfect wheel.

Five Considerations for Selecting the Perfect Wheel

So you've probably heard the saying, "You get what you pay for." In general, this is also true with pottery wheels. The exception is when you can **shop for, or negotiate a great price** on a great wheel.

Here's how to find a great deal. Search the internet. Compare prices. Check local retailers. Ask about sales and discounts. Look for discount packages that include other things you'll need like tools, clay, glazes or a splash guard.

In general, **expect to pay around $350 to $1400 for a new wheel, $75 to $1000 if it is used**.

If you want to get the perfect electric pottery wheel at a great price, first you need to determine what kind of wheel you need.

For example, if you're only going to be throwing small vases, you don't need a wheel with a 1 horse power motor.

If you aren't going to be throwing large pots, you can save money by going with a less powerful wheel.

If you want to save lots of money, consider a used pottery wheel. There are lots of pottery wheels out there collecting dust, just waiting for you to give them a good home. Just be sure to check the wheel out before taking it home. Ask to throw a pot on it before buying to be sure it functions well.

Tip: **Here is what to avoid at all costs!** Avoid buying a used wheel with a major mechanical problem unless you know how to fix it. If you spend $100 for a wheel that doesn't work, you're out $100. Better to spend a little extra up front to get one that will work well for you.

1 - Power

This one is pretty simple. How much horse power does your wheel have? Most wheels range between 1/4 and 1-1/2 horse power. Manufacturers will usually give you an idea of how much clay you can center on a particular wheel.

Here is a guideline for selecting speed. A 1/4 horse power motor is suitable for small pots. 1/2 horse power is more than enough for most potters. If you're making four foot tall vases you might want a 1 or 1-1/2 horse power motor.

2 - Quality

How smooth is the pedal? Does the wheel head twitch at low speeds or turn slowly and evenly? Is the motor quiet or noisy?

These three factors affect your throwing experience.

If you're making delicate porcelain vases you would want a smooth wheel motion.

If you're throwing pots at night while your 1 year old sleeps in the next room you would want a nice, quiet wheel.

3 - Features

Many potters use a **splash guard** to keep the water and slip from splashing everywhere. Is a splash guard included?

Is the work surface large enough to accommodate your tools? Could you easily use a table to provide space if it doesn't?

Do you want to **throw standing up**? Some potters find this much easier on their back. If so, could the wheel attach to a leg extension kit like the Brent Booties?

Are you left handed? Consider a wheel with a reverse switch if throwing counter-clockwise feels more comfortable.

Finally, what size is the **wheel head,** and can you attach removable bats to it? Larger pieces like plates and serving bowls require a larger wheel head.

4 - Portability

Will you need to move the wheel frequently?

Some free-standing electric pottery wheels such as the Shimpo Aspire Pottery Wheel can be very light and easily movable with only one person.

If you are working out of an apartment or have very limited space, a table top wheel like this might be the answer.

The Shimpo Aspire Pottery Wheel centers 20 pounds of clay and is also much less expensive to buy than larger wheels!

See this article for creative set up of pottery studios in small spaces.

On the other hand, if your wheel is going to stay in one place for many years a large, powerful, heavy wheel would be a good buy.

5 - Kid's Wheels

In general children under about the age of 13 will enjoy hand building pottery projects over wheel projects.

However, this depends on the individual child.

A rare few will be surprisingly patient and able to grasp the wheel.

Others will be interested, but will struggle to put together the complex steps involved in electric pottery wheel throwing.

In most cases, especially for very young children, a toy wheel such as the Alex Deluxe Pottery Wheel can offer a good introduction. A toy wheel can be inspiring. They can have fun and try what the adults are doing.

It's a great way to introduce the spinning concept. In general, however, don't expect much actual pottery to come off a toy wheel. **Also, remember to keep it fun.**

Tip: If you want to really challenge your own skills, and the skills of your fellow potters, have a competition to see who can actually throw something on a toy wheel!

How to Choose and Buy the Best Clay

Choose the right pottery clay to buy for your clay pot projects on the pottery wheel.

Choosing the right pottery clay can be challenging. When you're first learning, keep it simple. First we'll look at some definitions of clay. Then I'll share three easy questions you can ask to help determine which type of clay is right for you.

Introduction to Pottery Clay

What is Clay? - In technical terms clay is made up of very small particles of silicate created by the chemical weathering of rock. It is often found in lake or river beds, or in places where forces of erosion have carried and deposited it.

Clay For Pottery - In pottery terms, clay is a plastic (meaning able to bend and hold it's shape) combination of minerals that can be formed, and permanently hardened by firing.

My Definition of Clay - For me, clay is that amazingly sticky yet slippery, solid yet mold-able mud that makes all sorts of cool pottery possible.

It comes in a variety of colors from brown clay to white clay, red clay, cream clay, and speckled clay. It is soft when wet, brittle when dry, and extremely hard when fired.

Here are three easy question to help you determine the right clay for your pottery project.

Question 1 -
Are You Just Getting Started?

If you are new to making pottery on the wheel, here are a couple of things to look for.

1) Use a light colored clay. Red clays tend to stain clothing due to their iron content.

2) Use a smooth clay that has little or no grog in it. Grog is coarse, like sand.

It has it's place in pottery. It is used in clay to make it stronger and keep it from shrinking in the kiln.

However, when you are throwing for the first time, it can rub your skin like sandpaper and make it a lot less fun.

Question 2 -
At What Temperature Will You be Firing?

Firing pottery is one of the most fun aspects of pottery. It is important, however, to know what temperature the clay needs to be fired to. Clay firing temperatures are measured by pyrometric cones ranging from cone 022 to 10.

The three most common firing cones are 05 (low, earthenware), 5 (mid-range), and 10 (high, stoneware and porcelain).

Cone 05, or low-fire is usually best for beginners. It fires more quickly. More kilns can reach cone 05, and there are more commercial glazes available that fire at this temperature.

I fire at cone 5 (mid-range). It is still fairly user friendly, glazes are easy to come by, and the firing is faster than cone 10.

Many potters fire in the cone 9-10 range using gas or wood kilns. This provides unique opportunities for very durable pottery with exceptional glaze results.

Question 3 -
What Project are You Creating?

Your project determines the type of clay you will need. For smaller clay pot crafts to make for beginners a smooth clay of any firing temperature is good.

If you want to make pottery for use with food, higher temperatures tend to be better because they are more water tight.

Darker clays will tend to show through the glazes, whereas white clays don't influence the glaze as much.

How to Select Pottery Tools

To get started making your own pottery you'll need these 5 basic tools:

1) <u>Clay Wire</u>

2) <u>Sponge</u>

3) <u>Clay Knife</u>

4) <u>Rib</u>

5) <u>Clay Needle</u>

These can be purchased in a kit for around $13.00 or you can make most of them for even less.

Additional Tools

Other great tools to have are:

6) Trimming tools for finishing the bottom of the pot.

7) Carving tools for adding designs.

8) Stamps for imprinting textures.

9) Shammys for controlling water and finishing the rim.

10) Sponge on a stick for getting water out of the bottom.

11) Brushes of various coarseness.

12) Squeeze bottles for applying slip.

13) Large, small, and unique shaped ribs for shaping the pot.

14) Calipers for measuring pots, lids, and rims.

15) Ruler, also for measuring.

16) Throwing sticks for reaching into tall, skinny pots.

17) Paddles for shaping, thinning, and adding texture.

Making Your Own Tools

Here are a few ideas for homemade pottery tools:

1) **Cutting Wire** - Make a cutting wire by connecting heavy fishing wire between two ink pens or small dowels.

2) **Special Ribs** - Make a rib using scrap wood or an old music CD. Simply cut it and sand the edges to the desired shape.

3) **Free Shammy** - Make a shammy using a strip of plastic grocery bag. This is a great way to polish the rim of your pot. Just wrap it gently over rim while the pot is spinning.

4) **Stamp Roller** - Create your own stamp roller by rolling a slab of clay into a tube. When it's leather hard carve a repeating design into the surface. Bisque fire it, then roll it onto your clay pot projects.

5) **Pens** - I frequently sign my pots with ball point pens. The ink part doesn't work, but the tip is just right for incising a quality line into damp clay.

6) **Forks and Fabric** - Both are great for adding texture to damp clay surfaces.

Ceramic Equipment

Making pottery requires a lot of equipment. You can sort through various ceramic supplies quickly and easily in the following pages. Get valuable pottery equipment tips and advice.

List of Helpful Pottery Equipment

1) Ceramic Kiln

2) Pottery Wheel

3) Slab Roller

4) Clay Extruder

5) Glaze Mixer

6) Wedging Table

7) Pug Mill

As long as you have a wheel and a kiln you can make pottery. However, depending upon what you want to make will determine the other equipment you will need.

For example- If you are throwing solely on the wheel, you do not need a slab roller.

If you are using only store bought clay and not recycling any of your wasted clay, you do not need a pug mill.

If you are using smaller amounts of commercial glazes, you do not need a glaze mixer.

Finally, if you throw in a seated position, you do not need a pottery wheel leg extension.

Ceramic Kilns

Plan to buy or build an electric, wood fired, gas or raku kiln? Find free info about ceramic kilns and kiln manufacturers. Whether you're looking for used kilns, electric kilns for sale new, review your kiln buying plans, kiln firing temperatures, or getting started using a pottery kiln, this is the place to be.

Let's talk about the different types, brands and components of pottery kilns. First the different types.

Pottery Kiln Types

Wood Fired - I mention this first because this was the original firing method for pottery thousands of years ago.

It ranges from simple pit fires to intricate climbing kilns.

Regardless of the kiln structure, the fuel for the heat is wood. Wood firing is still very popular to this day because of the rich surfaces that it produces.

Gas Fired - A more modern version of the fuel burning clay kiln uses gas. This allows more control over the temperature and a cleaner burning kiln.

Gas is very popular because it still allows lots of option for creating rich glaze surfaces, without having to burn a ton of wood.

Electric - The newest form of kiln burns no fuel. It is heated by electric coils. It is very clean and easy to control.

Brighter colors can usually be achieved in electric kilns. However, electric kiln glazes tend to lack some of the richness of surface that can be achieved with gas and wood.

Raku - Raku is unique in that it involves multiple processes. First the pottery is heated to red hot (usually in a simple gas kiln). Then it is placed in another fuel such as newspaper or leaves to smolder. This smoldering creates very interesting surfaces.

Raku firing is really fast. It can be a great source of instant gratification in an art that is all about patience.

Pottery Kiln Brands

Here are some of the major brands of kilns. They are Skutt Kilns, Paragon Kilns, Olympic Kilns, Cress Kilns, Amaco/Excel Kilns, L&L Kilns and Cone Art Kilns. All kiln manufacturers build their kilns a little differently. L & L kilns are very popular right now, and several of the other brands have long histories of popularity as well.

Parts of the Kiln

Whether it uses wood, gas or electricity, every kiln has two structural components in common, insulated walls and shelves for holding ware.

Fire Brick - Specially insulated kiln bricks used to build clay kilns. These bricks are much more delicate than normal bricks. However, they can withstand extremely high firing temperatures.

They do an exceptional job of keeping the heat inside the kiln. Kiln bricks are available for sale where you buy other ceramic kiln supplies. You can repair most clay kilns when the bricks wear out by replacing them with new bricks as need.

Kiln Shelves - An important part of your kiln supplies is kiln shelves. They are specially constructed shelves that will withstand heat and support your pots in the high firing temperatures of the kiln. The shelves must fit with your pottery kiln design to maximize space while leaving a space of about 1" between the pottery kiln walls and the shelves.

Kiln furniture includes posts made of the same material as the shelves which hold up the shelves and allow you to arrange the shelves at varying height depending on the size of pots you are firing.

Chapter 2 - Throwing Pottery on the Wheel

Step 1 - How to Prepare Clay for Throwing

It is crucial to start off with great clay each time you make a pottery clay pot. Learn these easy techniques for preparing clay and you'll save yourself tons of time and energy.

Did you purchase your clay?

If so, it is pretty much **ready to use**. Clay companies have carefully formulated clay recipes. They process the clay using a pug mill so the prep work is done for you.

Many potters, including myself, will use store-bought clay straight out of the bag.

More meticulous potters will wedge their clay every time regardless of where they get it. If you make homemade clay, or are refreshing used clay be sure to wedge it thoroughly.

WEDGING- the process of kneading pottery clay to remove air bubbles, mix it to consistency, and align the clay particles to aid in throwing.

Two Wedging Techniques

1) Table Wedging

Take a ball of clay and slap it down on the table. Slice it in half with a wire clay cutting tool. Flip the top half upside down and slap it down hard onto the bottom half. Repeat this process as many times as it takes until the clay is smooth, consistent, and air bubble free. Be sure to **slap the clay down hard** to prevent air from getting trapped between the two pieces.

This is a great opportunity to check the consistency of the clay. Look at the cut surfaces. Run your finger across the surface. It should be smooth. It should have an even color (dark stripes usually imply dryer areas of clay). It should have no holes caused by air bubbles. If it isn't perfect, keep wedging. This is the foundation for your beautiful ceramic pot.

2) Spiral Wedging

This is a much more challenging method, but **worth learning**. It creates great results for you clay. Many potters prefer this technique because it lines up the flat, disc-shaped clay particles in a circular motion. This circular arrangement is perfectly suited to the circular motion of throwing on the wheel.

To spiral wedge think about doing the moon walk, only with clay. You're pushing the ball forward and downward into the table, while rotating the top of the clay backward toward yourself. **Push down with your right palm, while lifting and rotating backward with the fingers of both hands**. Then rotate the clay back toward you a 1/4 turn and repeat step one. Repeat this process until your clay is consistent.

When done correctly the clay will begin to form a spiral. **You'll find a rhythm** of rocking and pressing as you develop your technique.

Now, before you actually start to throw, you'll need to set up your wheel with some supplies.

Here's what you'll need:

- A good sized bucket of water, preferably a gallon or more.
- A second bucket for excess slip that builds up on your hands.
- A sponge, you can just throw this into the water bucket.
- A clay needle tool.
- A cutting wire, for removing you pot from the wheel.
- A wooden knife, for trimming excess off the bottom.

Optional supplies:

- A removable bat, so you can easily lift the pot off the wheel.
- Trimming tools, if you decide to trim the pot on the wheel.
- A sponge on a stick, to get water out of you pot.
- Other carving, cutting and decorating tools.

Step 2 - Centering the Clay on the Wheel

Centered clay is the foundation of pottery on the wheel. Remember that it takes time, but it will be well worth the time and effort it takes to learn to do this well.

Most people have to attempt to center AT LEAST 40 pieces of clay before they get it down, some need 100. Many quit before they get to that point, so whatever you do, keep going. Remember the third pillar of pottery: Patience. You can do it!

Okay, here we go.

1) Place a round ball of clay the size of your fist in the center of the wheel and press down on it with both hands. **It should stick**. That's how I like to do it.

Lots of potters will actually throw the clay onto the wheel. Try it. It's fun. With some practice you'll be able to hit the center.

Side Note: Some say this is why it is called pottery wheel "throwing". Others argue that it is called "throwing" because the origin of the word "to throw" is to turn.

2) In any case, once you have it stuck to the wheel, start the wheel spinning by pressing the pedal. Practice speeding it up and slowing it down.

When you're first learning pottery, practice stopping the wheel several times. You'll want to know how to do this later when it's time to take the pot off the wheel! Pat the clay gently toward the center as the wheel turns, keeping it as round as possible.

3) Now the fun begins! Get your hands wet and place them on the clay.

A note about water: While there are potters who can throw pots without using water, we humans need to get our clay wet when we throw it. This creates a thin layer of mud on the surface which keeps your hands from sticking to it. While you are throwing, water will spin off the clay and also be absorbed by your hands. Therefore, you must continuously add water to the surface of the pot as you throw.

In the beginning **be generous with the water**. As you continue to learn pottery and improve your skills you can use less water. This is beneficial, because too much water will soak into the clay and weaken the pot. However, in the beginning more water will help you get the hang of centering without your hands sticking to the clay.

4) Your body should be as close to the wheel as possible. **Body position is the most important thing** next to having good clay.

Your chair should be right up against the wheel. Your head should be directly over the ball of clay, elbows tucked into your ribs for support, hands touching each other and wrapped around the clay.

From your hands to your elbows and across you body should form a triangle. This triangle creates stability for your hands and makes centering a lot easier. You might be surprised how hard it is at first to control the clay. This is where good body position and a stable triangle will come to your aide.

5) The goal now is to center the clay making it perfectly symmetrical, with no wobbles, as it spins.

To do this, push the palm of your right hand against the side of the clay. Let your right thumb gently rest on top of the clay.

Then press on top of the clay with the blade of your left hand (like you're giving it a karate chop in slow motion). Your left hand should gently press against the pad of your right thumb to create the triangle of support.

Remember to re-wet your hands frequently so they don't stick to the clay. Slippery is good. Sticky is bad.

Pressing with both hands alternate the pressure, pressing down slightly harder with the left hand, then pressing inward slightly harder with the right hand. When you do this **the clay will change in shape**. This mixes and activates the clay and gets it ready for throwing.

6) Finally, press both hands with even pressure left hand still on top and right hand still on the side to center the clay. Remember correct body position, bracing your arms against your body. Also, remember to brace your hands against each other for more support!

The mound of clay should be slightly wider than it is high, like a hockey puck or better yet a thick cheeseburger, You'll know that the clay is centered when you can place your hands gently on the clay while the wheel is spinning and they don't wobble at all.

This is one of the hardest techniques to master when you are first learning pottery, so **if it isn't perfect right away, that's okay**. Take a deep breath, grab a snack, and try again.

Once you perfect centering you have the foundation of all pottery wheel throwing. When you're ready, go on to steps 3 and 4; creating a hole and opening up the form.

A small confession: I realize that the technique of centering can be very hard to understand without seeing it in person. Therefore, I strongly encourage you to use the free resources on the internet to watch people making pottery.

You can go to my website, www.pottery-on-the-wheel.com, under pottery videos, or YouTube has a ton of them, too. It helps a lot to be able to see the hand and body positions that I'm talking about here.

Troubleshooting

First, if you notice your claying taking on funny shapes, like a sharp lip or a tall cone in the center remember that your hands are creating that shape. Adjust your hand position slightly to change that shape to a nice hamburger bun or rounded off hockey puck.

Second, be sure to use very soft clay until you really have centering mastered. Hard, dry clay is much more difficult to center and you'll be worn out before you get to make your first pot.

Step 3 - Creating the Hole

This is where the fun begins in creating pottery. As we open up the centered ball of clay it begins to take on the shape of a pottery bowl. Follow these steps to make a hole in the center.

1) Spin the wheel at medium speed.

2) Using the thumb of your right hand press down gently into the center of the clay. **Remember good body position** when making pottery. Your chair should be close to the wheel, elbows braced against ribs, forearms can rest against your thighs. Use your left hand to support your thumb to prevent it from wobbling.

3) After you've gone a centimeter into the clay, pause and add some water so your thumb doesn't stick. Continue into the clay with your thumb until you are half an inch (the thickness of your thumb) from the bottom.

This is the same technique whether you are starting a small pottery bowl, a large coffee mug, a vase, or even a ceramic dog bowl. Whichever type of pot you are making, with the exception of plates, you follow the same process.

Step 4 - Open up the Form

1) Now, using the fingers of your right hand, **pull the clay open** into a bowl.

Be careful that you have plenty of water on the wall you are pulling against. You may need to stop and add some water even after you move the clay only a centimeter.

It should start out as a thick, short bowl at first. Only open up the clay about 1-2 inches total. If you pull too far, the walls of the bowl will fall off of the base. For now, leave the walls thicker (about 1 inch thick). We'll thin them and make them taller in a later step.

As always, use your other hand for strength and stability as you pull out. Grab a hold of your right hand with your left to give it support.

Great Job! Your clay is starting to look like a pot. In the next step you'll continue building the form of the pot. You're really creating pottery now!

Troubleshooting:

Your pot should be sturdy and evenly centered at this point. If your pot is wobbly or uneven one of these things may have gone wrong.

A) The clay walls became too dry while pulling the clay open. This causes your fingers to stick to one side of the pot more than the other. Solution: Use more water.

B) When creating the hole your thumb may have been off center. You'll know this because when you press your thumb into the clay it should not move from side to side. If you haven't pushed too far down, you can correct this by re-centering the clay and starting the hole again.

If you've already begun to open the pot and it has a good wobble, you'll want to remove the clay, re-wedge it, and start over.

When you're ready, go on to step #5, making the floor.

Step 5 - Finishing the Floor of the Pot

This is one of the wheel techniques that is often neglected. A well formed floor, however, can create dramatic results for your pot.

1) The Right Depth:

A thin floor is too fragile. A thick floor makes the pot too heavy. A good rule of thumb is for the floor to be 1cm thick, or the thickness of your little finger. Error on the thick side at first. As you improve you'll get a good sense of **just the right thickness for each pot.**

To measure the thickness of the floor, stop the wheel. Insert a needle tool into the floor of the pot until it hits the wheel head. Don't worry about the hole. It will fill in on the next step.

Before removing the needle from the clay, slide your index finger down the needle until it touches the clay. **Keep your finger in place** on the needle as you remove the needle tool from the clay. The thickness of your floor is the distance between your finger and the tip of the needle.

2) Compress the Clay:

With the pottery wheel spinning slowly press down gently on the floor of the pot using a sponge. Pressing through the sponge with your fingers, distribute the pressure evenly across the right half of the bottom of the pot (the 3 o'clock position on a clock face). This will strengthen it, thin it a little more (not too much!), and help prevent it from cracking.

It will take some practice to get the pressure correct so that the bottom of the pots stays flat. If you press too hard in one area you'll notice the floor will become more uneven.

A Note on Flooring: The floor is important regardless of what pottery design you are creating. For instance, when looking at a ceramic mixing bowl, often the first thing you see is the inside.

With pottery dinnerware it is even more important. On a ceramic plate, the floor makes up most of the pot. So, take an extra moment to make sure it is smooth, and that it fits the overall shape of your pot.

3) Shape and Smooth the Floor:

Finally, using the sponge again, create a good shape to the floor. **Pay special attention to the transition** between the floor and the wall. For a pottery coffee mug you would likely want a more squared off corner. However, for a pottery mixing bowl a rounded, gradual transition would be better. In fact, with good pottery mixing bowls you can't see where the floor ends and where the wall begins.

Great Job! Now we'll work on Pulling up the Walls.

Step 6 - Pulling up the Walls and Shaping the Pot

These two pottery techniques are where the magic begins. This is where a lump of clay becomes a work of art.

1) The First Pull

For the first pull, make a "C" shape with your left hand. Use your hand like a crab claw, fingers inside the pot, thumb on the outside. Drizzle some water over the rim using a sponge to coat the walls and prevent sticking.

Your right hand should act as the support, touching your left wrist or thumb to help stabilize it.

Starting at the bottom of the wall, squeeze your thumb and fingers gently together through the clay as the wheel spins.

A bulge of clay will form above where you are squeezing. **Slowly and steadily pull the clay upward through the wall toward the top of the pot.** As with most of the pottery techniques we have learned, add water as needed so you don't stick to the clay.

Continue pulling up, lessening the pressure as your fingers rise, until your thumb is half an inch from the top. Then, slowly release your grip. Leave some extra clay on the rim so you don't tear through it.

Tip: Any time that you feel you are losing control or feel you are sticking to the pot, just let go of the pot and rest for a moment. Add some water, check your walls for overly thin spots and start again where you left off.

Beginners tend to feel as though if they let go of the pot it will fall down. If that is true, then the pot is not going to survive anyway.

The magic of pottery is the moment when the clay begins to defy gravity. Just remember that you don't need to continually hold it up.

2) Thinning

Now that the walls are growing taller we'll use a different pottery technique, which allows your hand to reach further down into the pot. **We'll use both hands now.**

Your left hand goes inside the pot, while your right hand goes on the outside. Continue to use the fingers of your left hand as on the first technique. Replace your thumb on the outside with the finger tips of your right hand. Holding a sponge in your right hand, press your fingertips through the sponge against the base of the pot.

The sponge helps to prevent you from sticking to the pot. It allows you to throw longer without adding water.

Now, hold the sponge steady as the wheel turns. **Very slowly bring your hands up the side of the pot**. Press gently into the wall. Your left hand is mostly just supporting the wall from the inside. Most of the pressure will be with the sponge in your right hand. Again, leave the rim a bit thicker to add support to the walls. Be sure to keep the walls wet inside and out.

Repeat this pulling process until the walls are about 1 cm thick (thicker is okay on your first few pots). Later you'll work toward getting them about 3/4 cm thick. In some cases you'll go even thinner. This will enable you to create nice light-weight bowls, mugs and vases.

A Note about Pressure: You'll notice that at the bottom of the wall where the clay is thicker, it will require more pressure from your fingers. However, as you move toward the top of the wall you'll need a more and more delicate touch to keep from collapsing the walls.

3) Shaping

Finally, shape the walls of the pot. Use the same hand position as with thinning. Only now, depending on the shape of the pot press harder from the inside or outside. For a bowl, gently pull the entire wall open with the left hand, while supporting it on the outside with right hand.

For a vase you would push out the bottom of the wall and squeeze the neck inward. (see more about vases on the Advanced Projects page)

Great Job! It's really starting to look like a pot now. Take your time on this step. It's one of the toughest, but most important of the pottery techniques you will learn. It won't be perfect right away, so keep practicing.

If your rim is wobbly at this point, it's okay. In the next step we'll work on trimming and finishing the rim.

Step 7 - Finishing the Rim

When learning how to make pottery, this is a simple but important step. Finishing the rim is a two part process.

1) Cutting the Rim

The purpose of cutting the rim is to make it nice and even. If your rim is perfectly even, skip to step 2. If you have a little wobble that's okay. We'll fix it.

First, spin the wheel very slowly. Then position your left thumb and fingers in a "C" shape supporting the rim. The fingers are on the inside. The thumb is on the outside. This is the same hand position as your first pull.

Next, take a needle tool in your right hand **slowly cut into the rim of the pot**. Go far enough down the wall to make a full cut all the way around the pot. You want to remove all of the clay that is uneven without taking any more than necessary. Usually, a 1-2 cm strip of clay is all you'll need to cut off.

Note: When you begin to cut the rim, point the needle a little to the right, **with the direction of the spinning**. If you point it to the left, into the spinning, it will jab into the pot and ruin it. This tip applies anytime you're touching the pot with a finger or tool.

Once you've cut all the way through, **lift the cut piece off using your left hand**. Presto, the rim is even. Now it just needs a little refining.

2) Smoothing and Shaping the Rim

First smooth the rim with a sponge to remove the sharply cut edges. Support the rim with you left hand as in step 1 so it stays upright. Gently wrap the sponge over the rim to create more of a rounded shape.

You can vary the shape of the pot's rim to make it suitable for mugs or pitchers or other pots. You do this by adjusting the thickness and sharpness of the lip.

Way to Go!

If you've created anything resembling a pot at this point you are light years ahead of most people who only dream of making pottery.

You've proven that you can do it. I'm so proud of you. Keep going. You're almost there! Next Trim the Base and Cut the Pot Off the Wheel.

Step 8 - Trim the Base

Awesome Job! You're truly learning pottery wheel throwing. Just one more step and your pot is finished! It's time to cut the extra clay off the base and remove the pot from the wheel.

First, we'll remove any excess clay from the bottom of the walls. **Start by spinning the wheel slowly.**

Hold a needle tool in your right hand like you would hold a pencil. Notice how the bottom of the wall is thicker than the top?

With the needle, **cut into the wall at a 45 degree angle** about 1/2 inch from the bottom. Keep going until the needle is touching the wheel. Hold the needle in place until the wheel makes a full turn.

Now, stop the wheel and gently slice underneath the cut piece all the way around the pot. Remove the loose clay. This will create a nice undercut to the base and remove excess weight.

Use a damp sponge to **round out any jagged edges** where it was cut.

Congratulations! Using these pottery wheel throwing lessons you have officially thrown your first pot on the wheel.

Step 9 - Cut the Pot off the Wheel

Now, it's time to cut it free. It's very important to cut it off the wheel before it dries or it will crack.

Take a clay cutting wire in both hands. If the wire is too long you'll need to wrap it once around your fingers. Spin the wheel very slowly.

Be ready to stop the wheel if you need to. Practice stopping it a few times beforehand so you've got it down. Hold the wire tightly. Place your thumbs on the wire, pointing inward, so you have good control of it.

Hold the wire flat against the wheel head on the side of the pot that is farthest from you. As the wheel turns **slowly pull the wire under the pot** toward your body.

Tips: Keep the wire tight and flat against the wheel. The spinning motion will try to pull your right hand around the wheel to the left. Resist this pull.

Keep your arms straight across from each other. Pull steadily toward your body. Hold the wire tight until it come out from underneath the pot. You may have to jerk it a little to get it out from under the pot.

Once you've cut completely through, **stop the wheel.** Also, stop the wheel anytime you lose control of the pot.

Now it's time to let the pot dry to leather hard. When the walls are leather hard, about 3-4 hours, turn the pot over. Smooth the bottom with a damp sponge. For a more refined finish trim your pot on the wheel.

Finally, sign your name on the bottom with a clay needle or a ball point pen (it creates slightly smoother letters). Or you can optionally trim the base of your pot on the wheel to give it a more professionally finished look.

Congratulations! Way to go! Your pot is finished. Once it's dry it'll be time to fire and glaze it.

Chapter 3 - Trimming

Trimming- The process of carving your clay pot projects while they are spinning on the wheel. You can trim almost any part of a pot. Lids can be shaped, walls can be thinned, and a foot can be added to the bottom by trimming.

If you look at almost any tableware, whether it's a paper cup or a porcelain plate, you will see a small rim on the bottom of the container.

This small rim is the foot.

Trimming is how you add a foot to your pot.

The foot helps it to sit level on a table.

It also removes excess clay and weight from the pot.

A good example of this is in trimming the top of a lid.

In this pottery lesson we'll look at both how to trim a lid and how to trim a foot.

They both start off the same way, with re-centering the clay pot projects on the wheel.

First, a note on drying the pot.

Step 1 - Drying to Leather Hard

The very first thing you must do is dry your clay pot project until it is **leather hard**. Leave your pot exposed to the air to firm up. This generally takes between two and six hours, depending on the size of your pot and the temperature and humidity in the room.

The rim will usually dry the fastest. I recommend turning your pot upside down as soon as the rim and walls are dry enough to handle. The bottom of the pot is thicker and needs to be exposed to the air in order to dry properly.

Leather hard is just what it sounds like. Your pot should be the stiffness of leather in a shoe, slightly soft and pliable, but not wobbly, wet or sticky. This is important.

If your pot is too dry, carving will be difficult and you will be scraping hard clay and dust off your pot. It will dull your tools and it isn't a lot of fun.

If your pot is too wet, the trimmings will still be sticky. They'll stick back onto the pot and make a mess. This isn't a lot of fun either.

However, if your pot is just right, the trimmings will peel of in beautiful little spirals. They will curl off and away from your pot. Your tool will cut smoothly, and you will really enjoy trimming your pottery.

Step 2 - Re-Centering

Now that your pot is leather hard, it's time to re-center it on the wheel.

To re-center it, place the pot upside down on a clean wheel or bat. Place it as close to centered as you can. Then, start the wheel spinning slowly.

Using a clay needle tool gently move the tool toward the pot until it lightly touches the pot near the base, as shown in the photo. Notice how the needle is pointing with the spinning of the wheel (the wheel is spinning counter clockwise) not into the side of the pot..

This is very important to prevent the needle from stabbing into your pot. You just want the needle to graze along the side of the pot.

When the pot is centered, you will be able to scratch a perfectly even line all the way around it while the wheel spins.

If the pot is off center, you'll notice that the needle doesn't scratch all the way around the pot. It will only scratch on one side. This tells you to which side your pot is off center.

Allow the needle to scratch just a little bit. Then, stop the wheel. Rotate the wheel until the scratched portion is facing you. Push the pot gently away from you to move it closer toward being centered.

Repeat this process until you can incise a line evenly all the way around the pot.

Step 3 - Anchoring the Pot

Once you have your pot centered, you need to anchor the pot to the wheel.

Take a small wad of clay and break it into four cherry-sized pieces.

While holding the pot in place, gently press the clay balls down against the wheel alongside the pot.

Take care not to press into the side of the pot too much. This can distort your pot or push it off center.

Continue until all for balls of clay are secure. Then recheck your pot to make sure it is still centered. This can be done simply by spinning the wheel and holding your finger alongside the pot touching it lightly while it spins.

Step 4 - Trimming the Base

Now the fun begins. Start the wheel spinning.

Using a clay carving tool, begin to gently carve away thin layers of clay from the surface of your pot.

If you are trimming a lid, you'll be shaping

the clay to suit the vessel that the lid belongs to. This could be rounded, squared off, or pointed on top.

Use the smaller surfaces of the tool, removing the clay in thin layers.

If you find that the tool is catching on the clay, one of two things could be wrong. Either the tool is not sharp, or you are trying to take too much clay off at one time.

If this happens check the tool for sharpness and try trimming off very thin layers.

At times your pot may come loose from the anchors. If this happens, stop the wheel immediately. Re-center the clay and re-anchor it.

Tip: I usually place my other hand gently on top of the pot while I'm trimming it. I barely touch the pot, just allowing my fingers to graze it while it spins. This allows me to feel if the pot it coming loose or moving at all.

Always be aware of how thick or thin your pot is. This will help you to avoid carving through it.

Step 5 - Trimming a Foot

Up until this point the steps for a lid or a foot are the same. However, if you are trimming a foot, it requires a different shape than a lid.

To carve a foot into the bottom of your pot, begin by marking where you want the foot to be. This can be done using your needle tool or a carving tool.

This is important as it gives you a guide to prevent you from carving the foot off of your clay pot projects.

Then carve out a layer of clay from the center of your pot out to the inside of the foot. Carve as many layers as necessary to give your pot the shape and weight that you want.

Finally, carve off any excess clay to the outside of the foot. This will allow you to further refine the shape and weight of your clay pot projects.

Tip: If your clay is soft enough, you can gently smooth your finger along the edges of the foot as the wheel spins. This will polish the foot, leaving it really nice and smooth (unless you have a really rough clay).

That's it. Let your pot dry and you're ready to fire your pot.

Chapter 4 - Firing Pottery

Firing pottery is both exciting and challenging. Perfect your clay pot projects through firing. Follow the process here from throwing ceramic greenware pots to painting clay pots with glaze.

Lifecycle of a Pot

When the life of a clay pot begins, it's just a ball of clay in your hands. With a little practice, elbow grease, and mud, it becomes a pot. Until the pot is fired, it is called ceramic greenware.

Electric ceramics kiln being loaded with ceramic greenware.

Your greenware pot is then fired slowly to bake all of the moisture out of the clay. This first partial firing or bisque ceramics firing hardens the greenware so it can be handled without breaking. After the pot has been fired once it is called bisque or bisque ceramics.

Finally, your bisque is dipped, sprayed, or painted with pottery glazes. Once the glaze dries, it is fired a second time to a much hotter temperature. This is called the glaze firing.

At this point the clay particles fuse together or "vitrify", and the pot is "mature". Mature clay is highly water resistant and durable.

Note: Low fire pottery is less water resistant and durable than high fire pottery due to the additives that are required to help the clay to fuse at such low temperatures.

In this final firing the glaze also vitrifies and fuses to the clay. The glaze further increases the water resistance and durability of your clay pot project. When this firing is finished your pot is complete!

Right: Electric ceramic kiln being loaded with glazed pottery.

What is Firing?

Firing pottery- is the process of controlling the heat rise in the kiln to produce the desired results. This accomplishes two things for the pots.

First, it heats the pottery just to the point of maturity, bringing out it's highest quality and function. Second, it allows the potter to manipulate the fuels to create special glaze and surface effects.

When firing pottery, there are several ways to determine when the pottery has reached the maturation point. The most common and reliable method is with pyrometric cones.

Pyrometric cones are specially formulated cones of clay material designed to melt after they have experienced a certain amount of "heat work".

Heat work- is a combination of temperature and time.

Therefore, a cone fired over a longer time can melt at a lower temperature than a cone fired over a shorter time. This gives the potter a very accurate gauge of how the firing is going.

Many kilns also contain pyrometers which measure the actual temperature in the kiln. This provides a rough estimate of how the firing is progressing.

Finally, many potters have an eye for gauging the temperature in the kiln by the color of the glow on the pots. By looking into the kiln through a peephole you can see different hews of orange, which indicate different temperatures.

Tip: When firing pottery, always follow the kiln manufacturers safety recommendations. Use proper eye protection when looking into the kiln as the light can be damaging to the eye.

How to Fire Bisque Ceramics in an Electric Kiln

Bisque Ceramics-is the middle step in pottery. After the pot has been formed and dried it is then bisque fired. The bisque fire cooks off any residual moisture from the greenware and hardens the pot partially so it is ready to glaze.

Greenware- is any pottery that has been formed but not yet fired. Until it has been fired it can be turned back into clay simply by soaking it in water. Greenware is soft and wet after being thrown and is dry and brittle after it dries.

About Bisque

Bisque is more durable than greenware and is easier to work with when glazing. It is only partially fired, leaving the clay porous, which also helps it to absorb pottery glazes for a more durable finished pot.

Tip: There are two keys to successfully firing pottery bisque. First, dry the greenware completely before firing. Second, increase the temperature very slowly to allow any moisture to slowly release from the clay, rather than boiling and exploding your pottery.

The following is an overview of the bisque firing process.

Prepare a Cone Pack

At least two hours before you begin firing make a cone pack. To do this, form a bar of clay 2cm x 2cm x 10cm. Poke it full of holes with a clay needle, especially if it is recycled or homemade clay. This will prevent it from exploding in the kiln.

Place three pyrometric cones into the clay, cone 09, 08, and 07. Most bisque ceramics are fired to somewhere between cone 08 and cone 05. I fire all of mine to 08. Be sure that the cones are angled slightly (8 degrees) so that they'll curl to one side when they melt.

Load the Kiln

The great thing about ceramic greenware is that it isn't covered in glaze. You can pack the kiln very tightly without worrying about the glaze on the pots welding them together. Walls and rims can touch without any worries. They can even be stacked if done carefully.

Tip: Avoid stacking large, heavy pots on top of small, delicate pots. Several pots can be stacked if you put smaller, lighter pots on top.

If your kiln uses a kiln sitter, be sure to place a small 08 or 06 cone in it before loading. It's very frustrating to load the whole kiln and then have to unload it in order to get that one little cone in its place.

Place the kiln shelf posts into the kiln first. Then load the greenware around the posts. If you place 4" posts on a shelf try to find pots that are just under 4" to maximize kiln space.

Continue stacking pots and kiln shelves all the way to the top.

Important: Remember to position your cone pack where it will be visible through a peep hole. Make sure no pots are blocking it. You can place a piece of broken kiln shelf or fire brick under it if the peep hole is too high.

Fire the Bisque

When firing bisque ceramics, think like a tortoise, slow and steady wins the race. Leave the door propped open 2" and the peep hole plugs out for at least the first hour. Start at the lowest heat setting. After an hour, close the door and the peep holes. Continue to fire slowly until you reach cone 08. Turn off the kiln. Leave it closed and allow it to cool completely.

Cooling can take from 24-48 hours. Opening the kiln too soon can shock the ware and cause cracking. Once you turn the kiln off, it's best to forget about it for a day or two. When you do finally open the kiln, feel the pots on the top. They should be room temperature.

Important: Always follow the manufacturer's recommendations for operating your pottery kiln. Use proper eye protection when looking into the kiln peep holes to prevent eye damage.

More on Ceramic Kilns and Firing

Getting access to a ceramic kiln can be one of the biggest hurdles for a beginning potter. I know it was for me, especially once I left college.

I didn't appreciate the facilities that I had access to when I was in college. We had raku kilns, pit firing, gas kilns, gigantic front loading kilns, and several large electric kilns.

Over the years since then, I have considered myself lucky to have access even to any kiln, as long as I can fire my pottery. Even now, my kiln isn't technically mine. I'm borrowing it from a friend. She had been packing the kiln around for years looking for a chance to hook it up. I just happened to have the perfect spot for it with an all important 220 volt plug nearby.

So, we pooled our resources, and I'm babysitting her kiln. That's how pottery is. It becomes a community event, which makes sense because it's been that way for hundreds if not thousands of years.

Anyway, it's a great kiln. It's not computer fired or anything, but it fires right every time. It's an old Cress kiln with a classic kiln sitter.

Of course, today, computerized kiln controllers are the norm. They are very accurate and make it easy to control your firing temperatures and schedules.

Still, firing using just pyrometric cones is an accurate way to fire pottery. See how to use pyrometric cones in a kiln sitter below.

Firing Using a Kiln Sitter

A kiln sitter is a device that tells the kiln when to shut off. You place a small pyrometric cone between three levers and when it melts, the levers turn off the kiln.

It works much better than a pyrometer because the cone measures "heat work", which is time AND temperature, whereas a pyrometer only measures temperature. This gives you a very reliable measure of exactly how the pots have been fired.

(I always place a cone pack inside with different temperature cones. These cones confirm that the kiln sitter did, or did not, do its job correctly.)

My kiln also has a thumb wheel, which allows me to start the firing off slowly, and gradually work up to greater increases in temperature as the firing progresses.

It can also be fired faster or slower depending on what I am firing. For example, I always fire **bisque** very slowly, especially at the beginning.

It needs time to heat slowly so the moisture can escape from the clay gradually. This prevents pots from cracking and exploding. I fire the bisque firing on the slowest setting possible.

On the other hand, for **glaze** I will fire fairly rapidly. The moisture has all been cooked out of the clay in the bisque firing, so the coast is clear.

This works out well, since the glaze has to be fired to a higher temperature. If I had to fire it slowly it would take two days just to heat the kiln, let alone waiting for it to cool.

Soaking the Kiln

Also, when firing glazed pots, I always **soak** the ceramic kiln for an hour before turning it off. Soaking is when you hold the temperature in the kiln at its highest temperature before you allow it to cool.

Soaking is good for glaze because it allows it to even out before cooling. It allows any blisters and bubbles a chance to smooth out before the glaze hardens and preserves them forever.

Soaking is the trickiest part of using a kiln sitter. The sitter will turn the kiln off when the cone melts. So to soak the kiln I have to turn it back on for an hour at a low temperature to "hold" the top temperature or "soak" the kiln.

The kiln has to be monitored closely toward the end of the firing. If the sitter turns off and the ceramic kiln begins to cool for an hour or two, the valuable effects of soaking may be lost.

By the way, I always allow the kiln to **cool for 48 hours after any firing.** Unless you are in a major, desperate rush to finish your pots, you don't want to open a hot kiln.

The shock to your pottery from rapid temperature change is not good for it. Besides, the mental game of checking the kiln every hour, and then trying to decide how cool is cool enough to risk it, can waste a lot of time and energy.

For any firing under cone 6, you can be sure that 48 hours is enough time for it to cool. In the mean time, go make some more pottery.

Ceramic Kiln Firing Schedules

Regardless of whether I am firing bisque or glaze, I like to fire over night. The reason for this is that, as I mentioned about, with a kiln sitter it is important to closely monitor the end of the firing. The rest of the firing progresses pretty automatically.

Bisque Firing Schedule

For a typical bisque firing I would set the kiln on the slowest firing setting.

Here's an example of how a cone 08 bisque firing would progress:

8pm - Make a cone pack with a cone 09, cone 08, and cone 07 in it, and load the kiln.

11pm - Turn the kiln on with the lid propped open 2 inches and the peephole plugs removed.

12:30pm - Close the lid and put the peep hole plugs in so the kiln is completely closed.

Let the kiln fire over night.

7:30am - Look through peep hole to check cone pack. If cone 09 has fallen, check kiln every 20 minutes until cone 08 has fallen. If cone 08 bends and kiln sitter hasn't turned off, turn kiln off manually.

Allow your ceramic kiln to cool for 48 hours before opening.

Open the kiln and glaze the pots.

Glaze Firing Schedule

For a glaze firing I set the kiln on the fastest setting. Here's an example of how a cone 5 glaze firing would progress:

8pm - Make a cone pack with a cone 4, cone 5, and cone 6 in it, and load the kiln.

11pm - Turn the kiln on with the lid propped open 2 inches and the peephole plugs removed.

12:00pm - Close the lid and put the peep hole plugs in so the kiln is completely closed.

Let the kiln fire over night.

7:30am - Look through peep hole to check cone pack. If cone 4 has fallen, check kiln every 20 minutes until cone 5 has fallen. If cone 5 bends and the kiln sitter still hasn't turned off, turn kiln down to lowest setting and soak for one hour.

Using the lowest setting keeps the ceramic kiln from cooling too rapidly. It's usually just enough to hold the temperature steady.

After one hour of soaking, turn kiln off manually.

Allow your ceramic kiln to cool for 48 hours before opening. Open the kiln and play with the beautiful pots.

Keep in mind that you can do a lot more with your firing by customizing your firing schedule, especially with a computerized kiln. On the other hand, an experienced potter can fire a kiln by monitoring the cone pack inside the kiln and little else.

My best tip: If in doubt fire a small test load first. It's better to ruin 3 pots than 30. Besides that, fire often and you'll learn fast.

Chapter 5 - Glazing Pottery

The most exciting part of pottery is glazing.

This is your opportunity to add color, flare, creativity, and durability to your ceramic creations.

When firing your pottery in an electric kiln, there are four main factors to consider.

We're only discussing electric kiln for now because they are the most commonly used, the most readily available, and the simplest to learn initially.

The four factors are

- Firing Temperature

- Type of Glaze

- Protecting the Bottom

- Method of Application.

You could spend a lifetime experimenting with just these four different factors. When you're ready, learn how to use pottery glazes that will bring your pots to life.

To help keep things simple for now, let's focus on our four main glazing factors.

Tip: Keep a ceramic journal to document your techniques, results, and experiences as you go.

Firing Temperature

When glazing pottery, **firing temperature is very important**. Pottery glazes are designed to work well when fired to specific temperatures. Fire too cool and the glaze will be chalky and won't attach to the pot. Fire too hot and it will melt, drip and crack.

The important thing to remember is to select a glaze that is designed to be fired to the same temperature as your clay. This helps you to achieve a good "fit" between pot and glaze. Commercial clays will indicate what "cone" they should be fired to.

Pyrometric cones measure how much heat is being absorbed by the pot. They range from the lowest, cone 022, to the highest, cone 10.

Cone numbers from lowest to highest:

022, 021, 020, 019, 018, 017, 016, 015, 014, 013, 012, 011, 010, 09, 08, 07, 06, 05, 04, 03, 02, 01, 1, 2, 3, 4, 5, 6, 7, 8, 9, 10

Left: Melted cone. A kiln sitter, after firing, holding a correctly melted pyrometric cone. This indicates that the kiln fired to the correct temperature or "cone".
Right: Un-melted cone. A kiln sitter, before firing, holding an un-melted pyrometric cone.

Type of Glaze

Once your have determined the firing temperature of your clay it's time to select your glaze. This is where you get to decide how your pot will look. Will it be red, green, or brown? Will it have a glossy or matte finish? Will it be thick, thin or drippy?

When you're starting out I recommend using a non-toxic, commercially prepared glaze.

These are easy to use glazes, ready to apply out of the jar.

The benefit is that the glaze has already been painstakingly formulated and tested for you.

This gives you a chance to focus on your glazing techniques and firing skills.

Once you have those mastered, you can experiment with formulating your own glaze recipes.

Protect the Bottom of the Pot with Wax

So your pot has gone through the bisque firing and it is ready to be glazed. Waxing is the first step before we apply the glaze.

When fired, glaze actually melts. If there is glaze on the bottom of your pot, when it melts it will fuse your pot to the kiln shelf that your pot is sitting on. This makes a nasty mess, ruining the pot and damaging the shelf.

Therefore, before covering it with glaze we'll **wax the bottom of the pot**. There are two ways to do this.

The best method is to **melt wax in a pan** on a low temperature. Then dip the pot gently into the wax. The wax should come about 1/4 inch up the side, usually just enough to coat the foot of the pot.

You'll have to add small amounts of wax as you go to keep the level at 1/4 inch. Be careful not to overheat the wax as it is flammable.

Tip: Find an old frying pan that you won't miss and designate it as your waxing pan. The wax is very difficult to remove from a nice pot once you've started melting it. Plus, if you let the wax cool in the pan when you're done, it'll be ready for you at just the right level next time you're glazing.

The second method is **wax resist.** This is a liquid wax that requires no melting. It is great if you don't want to deal with the heating process.

However, it's more tedious to apply and it tends to stick to everything, like your fingers and the sides of your pot. I generally reserve this wax for other types of decorative work.

When your glazed pot is dry, sponge off any glaze that remains stuck to the wax. When you fire the pot, the wax will simply burn off, leaving the bottom of your pot clean and glaze-free.

Applying the Glaze

Here are four different ways to apply the glaze to your pot.

Dipping:

The simplest method of glazing is to dip the whole pot into a bucket of glaze. This method is much quicker than painting clay pots with a brush. To dip, hold your thumb on the rim of the pot and your fingers underneath on the waxed bottom. Dunk the pot into the glaze. Be sure the glaze covers the whole pot, inside and out.

Lift it out of the glaze upside down and shake it to remove excess glaze. Set it upright to dry.

There will be a bare spot on the rim where your finger was. Dab a small drop of glaze onto the rim where your finger was to fill it in.

Tip: The thickness of the glaze on the pot is very important. Small differences in thickness can completely change the color and characteristics of a glaze. I usually have to add a little water to commercial glazes. You can use a hydrometer to measure the water content of a glaze to help get consistent results.

Over time, you will get a good sense of how thick a particular glaze should through experience. Just by stirring and dipping pots into the glaze you can tell if it is too thick or too thin. But if you want to get precise results every time, use a hydrometer and record the results in a glaze journal.

Some commercial glazes are formulated for brush application only. Still, I have used many of these to dip pots with good results, but they don't all work. Also, some glazes are specifically formulated for use in dipping.

Pouring:

If you have a limited quantity of glaze, or have an oddly shaped pot that will not dip well, you can pour the glaze over it. All you need is enough glaze to cover the pot and a wide bowl to catch the drips.

This technique takes some practice to get the coverage right. **The key is to plan ahead.** It is usually best to pour the inside of the pot first. Pour glaze into the pot and rotate it until the inside is fully covered, then dump the excess glaze out.

For the outside of the pot, turn it upside dow. Pour glaze steadily over the surface, rotating the pot quickly until all areas are covered.

Try to minimize excessive overlapping of glaze. Some overlap will be unavoidable.

Painting:

Painting clay pots with glaze is especially effective when you only have a small amount of glaze or when you are creating a specific design on the pot. The manufacturer will specify how many coats you need to apply. Usually, it is two to three.

If you are painting clay pots with glaze in a design, be aware that glazes become fluid when they melt. Your design may be blurred or ruined in the firing. Test your glaze first, or check with the manufacturer. If you are doing very detailed designs you'll likely want to explore other options for painting like using slips, stains, or engobes.

Tip: Always be sure to stir your glaze thoroughly before applying.

Spraying:

Spraying is a very effective and efficient way to glaze your pottery. The main drawback is that it requires a sprayer, compressed air, and a vented spray booth. It also requires cleaning the sprayer.

However, it certainly has its benefits. Not only does spraying provide great opportunities for even coverage, it also allows you to create interesting surface effects by layering different glazes one over the other.

Experiment with these different glazing technique. Find one that suits you, and then push the limits of what you can do with it.

More Pottery Glazing Techniques

Here are some more specific techniques for glazing. Use these unique techniques to bring your clay pot projects to life with richer colors and textures.

So far, we've covered four common methods for application of glaze: dipping, pouring, brushing, and spraying.

Now we'll take a deeper look into some more creative techniques. One thing to remember is that although we are learning how to use store bought glazes, you can also learn how to make your own glazes. But that lesson is for a more advanced book. For now, let's look at various glaze characteristics and what they can do for the surface of your pots.

What Else Can You Do with Glazes?

Surface:

Surfaces can range from shiny gloss to earthy matte.

Effects:

A wide range of visual effects can be achieved in the surface of the glaze.

For example, crystal glazes have a prismatic, crystalline effect on the surface.

Other glazes create speckled, mottled, and uniform surface effects on your pots.

Colors:

There are endless arrays of pottery glazes in existence. Just flip through a ceramic magazine and you'll see that glazes come in every color of the rainbow.

Colors tend to be brighter at the lower firing temperatures. Bright reds are difficult to achieve, but they are possible, especially at lower temperatures. Higher temperatures tend to encourage more earthy colors.

Textures:

Some glazes will be intentionally drippy, while others are designed to crack, called "crazing", or to leave patches of bare clay, called "crawling". With many glazes, thicker areas will be a completely different color than thinner areas. This gives an incredibly rich, activeness to the surface of the pot.

One example would be with clay coffee mugs. If you imprinted a pottery stamp into the handle of a ceramic coffee travel mug, the rim, the edges of the handle, and the raised portions of the pottery stamp image would be high-lighted by the mottled variations of the glaze.

Now, let's look at different application techniques.

Wax Designs

Wax allows you to create textural contrast on your pots by leaving parts of it unglazed. This is done by applying wax to certain areas of your pot. It's similar to the technique of waxing the bottom of the pot to keep it free of glaze.

Wax resist is a liquid wax that requires no heating. You can paint your pots with it to create a pattern before glazing. Paint designs stripes, lettering, or images with the wax. Then, when you apply the glaze the wax repels the glaze leaving bare clay.

Tip: Be sure to let the wax dry thoroughly before glazing. Otherwise, the liquid wax will get in your glaze and on your fingers and create a mess. Also, be sure to wipe any excess glaze off of the surface of the wax with a damp sponge before firing.

You can also draw on your pot with wax crayons for a similar effect.

Layering

Layering glazes is a great way to create interesting new results for your pottery using glazes that you already have. You can completely cover the pot in two different glazes, or you can dip half in one glaze and the other half in another glaze. Where the two glazes overlap they will mix, creating a third color.

Tip: Dip the rim of your coffee mug in a different color to give it unique contrast.

Stains

Stains are pure color that can be sprayed or brushed over or under the glaze to add details, and color. You can also create speckles on your pot by splattering stain over the glaze with the bristles of a toothbrush.

Tip: Stains tend to move with the glaze when it melts, which will cause intricate designs to blur, so test your stain first before creating a very intricate design.

Underglaze

Underglaze is a colorant, such as stain, that is mixed with clay to make it more stable. This prevents it from running and blurring like a stain is prone to do when applied with a glaze. Underglaze got its name because it is applied to the raw bisque "under" the glaze.

Sgraffitto

Sgraffitto involves covering the pot with a stain or underglaze and scratching through it to reveal the clay underneath. It is first done on greenware, then bisque fired, and finally glazed over with a light or clear glaze. Sgraffitto is excellent for fine detail and bold contrasts.

Intaglio

Intaglio creates an antiqued effect on your clay pot. It differs from sgraffitto in that you carve or etch into the greenware first. Then, you fire the pot to bisque. Next, you brush or sponge stain into the surface of the carved design. Finally, you wipe the excess stain away from the surface with a sponge. The carved areas retain the stain, creating an interesting antiqued effect.

Final tip: Test and play with pottery glazes at every opportunity. Throw 4" tall by 2" wide cylinders and test different glaze combinations and techniques on them. Keep track of your experiments in a ceramic journal so you can re-create them later. Number your pots on the bottom with a corresponding description in your ceramic journal to stay organized.

Chapter 6 - Beginning Pottery Projects

Here are a few simple beginning projects including bowls, vases, and mugs for anyone just getting started on the wheel.

If you're new to pottery it's best to start off with the previous 10 step lesson on Throwing Pottery on the Wheel. This will teach you the basics of making pottery.

Then come back here and you can try out some of the specific projects detailed below.

Bowls and Vases

The easiest projects to make when learning how to make ceramics are bowls.

Bowls are the easiest thing to make because the spinning of the wheel naturally wants to pull the clay out and open into a bowl shape.

The coolest thing about bowls is that for all of their simplicity, they are so useful.

We use hand made pottery bowls every single day in my house for soup, cereal, rice, pasta, fruit, and more.

I recommend starting out with a small bowl first. Once you feel confident with that, move up to bigger bowls. After bigger bowls, move on to vases. From there, the sky is the limit.

On your first few projects remember, just have fun with it. Your hands have a lot to learn.

Take your time. Don't be afraid to make mistakes. Sometimes it helps to watch another beginner so you don't feel like you're the only one learning.

I recommend watching beginning pottery videos online anytime you need some encouragement. You may get some laughs, too, or discover a specific technique that you've been missing.

How to Make Ceramic Bowls

From small bowls to intricate teapots, **most pots start with the same three steps**. First, center the clay. Next, open a hole in the clay. Third, pull up the walls.

From that point, most projects branch off in their own direction.

When making a bowl, pull the walls straight up on that first pull. Second, thin the walls until they are about half an inch thick. Then, smooth and round out the rim. Finally, **with one slow, steady motion stretch the walls outward into a nice bowl shape**.

Note: The walls will thin as you stretch them outward, which is why you leave them half an inch thick when you pull up your walls.

To accomplish this stretching, use the same hand position as when you are thinning the walls. Your left fingers go inside. Your right hand holds the sponge on the outside. Rather than your right hand doing the pushing, **your left hand does all the pushing from the**

inside, while your right hand merely supports the wall from the outside.

*Tip: Once the walls have been stretched out into a good bowl shape **try to avoid more thinning and shaping**. The walls are not as strong when they aren't straight up and down and may collapse. Slight refinements to the shape, however, are usually safe to do.*

*On the other hand, it's good to push the boundaries from time to time. Especially when you are first learning, **you want to see how much the clay can handle**. So play with it. See just how tall, how wide, or how thin you can make those walls before they collapse.*

If you do collapse a bowl or two or ten, don't worry. You learn from it. Just think of it as a good experiment.

How to Make a Vase

Of all the pottery projects you can learn, the vase is one of the simplest yet most varied. Vases can be tiny or they can be huge. They can be tall, short, fat, skinny or any combination of the four.

Depending on the size, they can be fairly easy or extremely difficult to throw. We'll start with a fairly easy small vase.

Practice it a few times. Then, I'd encourage you to expand your skills and try some tiny ones as well as some big ones.

Shaping a Vase

Once you can throw a centered cylinder, you can throw a vase.

To make a vase you're going to start with a basic cylinder. To throw a cylinder follow the basic beginning lesson until you have a tall, narrow shape, about 3" wide by 5" tall.

There are two simple steps to transforming the cylinder into a vase.

First, push out the lower half of the wall to form a rounded bottom on the vase. Then, squeeze in the neck to give it an elegant curvature.

The vase in the photo is an example of a simple vase with a little bit of alteration. As you can see, the rim has been altered by hand to add a scallop to it.

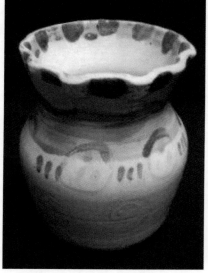

Side note: This can be done by simply pulling out on the rim with one finger, while you support the rim on both sides with the fingers of your other hand. Then slowly work your way around the pot.

Tips:

1) To push out the bottom, be sure the walls are wet on the inside so your fingers don't stick. Push very gently from the inside while supporting the pot from the outside. (Remember, a little pressure goes a long way.)

2) To squeeze in the neck, use your first finger and thumbs to create four points of contact. You can even use the knuckle of your second finger to make six points of contact on the neck of the vase.

Wet the outside of the walls first. Then gently squeeze in on the neck, about 2/3 of the way up the pot. Again, a little pressure goes a long way.

3) Finally, to finish it off, you can flare out the rim a little. Be careful not to fuss with the pot too much after you've shaped it. Once it has been shaped it will be much more delicate than when it was a straight cylinder.

Note on Vase Shapes: The difference between vase shapes depends on the height of each vase, as well as the ratios between the neck, the rim, and bottom of the vase.

Follow the 9 steps to remove your vase from the wheel, trim it and dry it. When you have finished your vase and dried it completely, bisque fire it, then decorate it with glazes and glaze fire it.

Experiment with different vase sizes and shapes until you find some that you really love.

How to Make a Coffee Mug

Once you're ready to try something more challenging, learn how to make clay coffee mugs.

While it may look hard at first, a mug is just a small vase with a handle.

Remember, in pottery your pots don't have to be perfect. You don't have to know how to do every project.

Just choose the projects that you enjoy and practice them over and over until you love the results. Then, when you're ready to try something new, go for it!

Clay coffee mugs are one of my favorite things to make and to use There is nothing like the experience of drinking coffee from one of your own handmade mugs..

Learn how to make your own mug in the pages below.

Once you've mastered making your own mugs and adding handles to them, a whole bunch of pottery possibilities opens up.

 The opportunities for creativity and variation are amazing for such a simple, functional pot.

In the photo is one example of an interesting mug variation.

A hand pulled handle take a little more practice than the coil handle I'll show you on this page, but it's worth learning when you feel ready.

This tan mug has a carved handle.

Here's how it was done. An extra thick handle was attached in the same way as we'll attach the coil in the instructions below.

The handle is allowed to dry a little to harden up. Then the excess is carved away, leaving the unique hand carved handle design.

The texture on the mug was carved into the clay with a fork, while the clay was leather hard.

It was then stained, wiped off the surface, and finally glazed. So, you can see about 4 different techniques in action just in one simple little mug.

Okay, so let's learn to create a mug.

The main challenge in making pottery coffee mugs lies in the handle. Therefore, that is where we'll spend the majority of our time. But first, we'll make the mug so it has some time to dry.

The Mug Body

To make a mug you'll first throw a cylinder five inches tall and three inches wide. Straight walls will work fine, or you can curve the walls a bit for a more interesting shape. Return to the Throwing Pottery on the Wheel chapter to learn how to throw a basic cylinder.

Once you have created the mug body, remove it from the wheel. Let it dry a few hours until the rim is dry enough to touch. **Turn your pot upside down** and smooth the bottom. Let it dry another hour or two until the whole thing is leather hard (or trim it on the wheel once it is leather hard).

While you're waiting for the pot to dry to leather hard you can start the handle.

Tip: You want to add the handle as soon as possible. You have to dry the pot a little or it will be mushy and fall apart when you are holding. But, if it gets too dry the handle won't adhere as well and the chances of your handle cracking off are greater.

It's a fine line, but a little softer is better than a little too dry. Also, if you run out of time before you get your handle on, just wrap your mug body tightly in plastic and it will keep for days. You can return and add your handle when you have the time.

The Handle

Take a ball of clay the size of a small peach. **Form it into a coil** by rolling it on the table until it forms a long rope. Work both hands back and forth down the length of it to keep it even.

Stop when the coil is a half an inch thick. Look at your mug and decide where you want to attach the handle. Look at pictures of mugs to get ideas. Most handles are attached at least a centimeter down from the rim and at least a centimeter up from the base.

The two most common shapes are a basic "C" shape, or the "EAR" shape. For this lesson we are doing a "C" shaped coil handle. Hold your coil up to your pot to measure how long it needs to be. Cut the coil to the right size using a clay knife or needle tool.

Make sure there is enough room for two fingers to fit into the handle

Keep in mind that, depending on the type of clay you use the handle with shrink about ten percent when it is fired.

You can leave the handle perfectly round, or you can use a rolling pin or small pasta roller to further shape the handle. You can give it any profile you like from triangular, to diamond, or even an indentation.

Note: the handle in the photo on the next page is a hand pulled handle. You can see how the shape is indented in the middle to make it easy to grip with your thumb. This is just one example of how you can modify the profile of your handle.

Next, bend the handle into a "C" shape so it's ready to go on the mug. Finally, let the handle dry alongside your mug body for about an hour so it will firm up a bit.

Attaching the Handle

Use a needle tool or toothbrush to "score" or roughen up, the two spots on the mug where you will attach the handle.

 Do the same to the ends of the handle.

Add a blob of "slip" or clay mud (leftover from your throwing), to the two spots on the mug that you just scored.

This will act as glue to hold the handle in place.

Then, press the handle onto the mug firmly.

Be sure to support the wall from the inside with your other hand so it doesn't collapse or crack.

If your handle doesn't survive the attachment process, for example, it cracks or you accidentally squish it, that's okay. Just cut it off with a clay knife, right where it attaches to the wall, and make another handle. While you're making your new handle, be sure to cover your pot with plastic so it doesn't get too dry.

Finish the Mug

Way to go! You're almost finished making your first of many handmade clay coffee mugs. To finish the pot, smooth the edges around where the handle was attached, using a damp sponge or brush.

The key with clay mugs it to dry them slowly. If they dry too fast, your handle may crack. If you've created an "EAR" shaped handle dry your mug upside down to keep the handle from drooping. Also, dry it slowly by covering it loosely in plastic for several days.

An additional trick is to paint wax resist around the joints where it is attached to the mug. This will force those areas to dry much more slowly, reducing the chances of cracking.

It usually takes 6 or 8 handles to start feeling confident with them, so keep at it. Just think, before long you'll be making clay coffee mugs like a pro and everyone will be begging you for one.

Keep in mind this is only the beginning of your journey. Focus on the basics and get them down. Once you've done that, the possibilities for creating interesting pottery are endless.

Final Note

Anyone can do pottery. The difference between those who do and those who don't comes down the Three Pillars of Pottery at the beginning of this book: **Supplies, Instruction, and Patience**.

The instruction is provided in this book, on the pottery-on-the-wheel.com website, and all of the free videos and information available on the internet.

If you can acquire the basic supplies, the only other thing you need is patience, and honestly, you only need a little bit of that. Believe me, I'm one of the world's least patient people, so I understand. I want everything to happen yesterday and to be perfect the first time.

But, patience really just means **"KEEP TRYING"**. Do it as many times as it takes. You cannot fail unless you quit.

Armed with those three pillars, your success is guaranteed!

Additional Resources

For additional projects, lessons and tips visit my free website at www.pottery-on-the-wheel.com. It includes videos that teach you how to throw pottery on the wheel as well as Intermediate and Advanced projects.

There is even an Artist's Page where you can post pictures of your work and tell other potters about yourself.

Thanks for reading, and Happy Potting.